Praise for *Seven L*

How does it feel to be desperate…wanting help, wa.... _ r something good to happen, and needing an uplifting hand to clear your difficulties? Felicita "Terry" Robinson found the solution— reaching out to God by writing her prayers. By this simple act of faith, she received guidance and solutions to her problems. God knows our needs but we must first ask [for] His help. In Matthew 21:22, Jesus said: *"…And everything you ask in prayer, believing, you shall receive."* Terry demonstrated her faith, and in this book, illustrates how we also can reap blessings from our Heavenly Father who loves and desires to reward us accordingly.

—Fay Massie, freelance writer and editor

Terry has received a marvelous gift from heaven in response to her 'Seven Letters to Heaven' and is now selflessly sharing it with the world. It is our responsibility to further share this gift with others by using our God-given talents. Thank you Terry and it is my intention to use my radio programs to do the same.

—John Blake
The Caribbean Experience
The Worldbeat Experience
WHUR-FM
96.3 MHZ
Washington DC

"The righteous cry out and the Lord hears and delivers them out of all their troubles."—Psalm 34:17
Without a test there is no testimony—Robinson takes us on her personal journey of tests with poems and prayers in her Seven Letters to Heaven.

—Beverley East, author of Reaper of Souls,
a novel of the 1957 Kendal Crash

SEVEN LETTERS
TO
HEAVEN

SEVEN LETTERS TO HEAVEN

A True Story of Faith and Answered Prayers

Felicita "Terry" Robinson

iUniverse, Inc.
New York   Bloomington

Seven Letters to Heaven
A True Story of Faith and Answered Prayers

iUniverse books may be ordered through booksellers or by contacting:

iUniverse
1663 Liberty Drive
Bloomington, IN 47403
www.iuniverse.com
1-800-Authors (1-800-288-4677)

ISBN: 978-1-4502-2920-3 (sc)
ISBN: 978-1-4502-2919-7 (dj)
ISBN: 978-1-4502-2918-0 (ebk)

Library of Congress Control Number: 2010906292

Printed in the United States of America

iUniverse rev. date: 06/25/2010

My sincere thanks to Sandra

Encouragement creates a pathway
to seemingly impossible dreams
—F"T"R

Preface

Why did I want to share this personal story? The simple answer is: my dear friend Sandra Ginyard encouraged me to do it. But to put things in their proper perspective, the Lord, in a very roundabout way, used her as His messenger to plant the idea into my mind.

My very personal letters of prayer, written to God while I was in Jamaica, had been sitting in the back of my Bible ever since my arrival in the United States in December of 1984. I knew they were there but except for the first couple of months in 1985, I never thought much about them until that day in 1991 when Sandra invited me to lunch. She had been the first person to befriend me on my job in Washington, DC in April of 1985. We have been friends ever since, and our lunch that day, in the cafeteria at the office, was just an impromptu get-together.

We had finished eating when she told me that she had something for me in her car. We walked together to the parking garage, and she took out a book from the trunk of her car. She handed it to me, saying, "You are the person to whom I am to give this book." She further explained that it was a book of poems that had been written by a woman who had not been a writer, but who got up one morning and started writing poems of a religious nature. The book had been her first published work. I quickly glanced through the pages of simple, yet moving poems, and immediately thought of the letters of prayer in the back of my Bible. I have no idea why they came into my thoughts at that time, but they did.

I said to Sandra, "I could do something like this."

She looked at me and repeated her statement, this time with conviction: "That's why you are the person to whom I am to give this book."

That evening, I rushed home and read the letters that were in my family Bible. While reading them, I recalled when they were written and why. I had composed them during a very busy four-month period of my life in Jamaica, prior to the relocation of my family to the United States. I also remembered that the good Lord had answered all of those prayers in one way or another. I thought to myself, *If that woman could publish her book of religious poems, perhaps I could share some of these simple letters with others. My story might just help someone who needs encouragement and inspiration.* These thoughts were so new to me, because never in my wildest dreams had I ever thought of sharing these personal letters with anyone.

I selected seven of the letters that had best captured my four-month experience and immediately started on the outline of my story. I worked feverishly into the night, as if I were on a mission. By the next day, I had completed my first rough draft (and one of many) of *Seven Letters to Heaven.*

Thanks to Sandra for revealing God's will to me in that simple statement: "That's why you are the person to whom I am to give this book." I could not be more convinced that sharing my story was the Lord's plan for me. This plan, however, was put on hold for several years, as I got caught up with the distractions of daily living; but I knew that someday I would finish this task.

I would like to thank my dear husband, Gary, for getting me to that someday. He spent the last ten years constantly reminding me that I had a book to complete. He also read and edited many revisions; sustaining and nourishing me during the times when I totally immersed myself in completing the book. My humble gratitude goes to Fay Massie for her generous and invaluable comments and advice. Her useful feedback pushed me to reveal more of my innermost thoughts and experiences, which helped the story to come alive. Special thanks to Teia Thompson-Brown as well, for patiently responding to all my questions on formatting during the last month of the completion of my book. Not to be left out either is the feedback that I got from my two children: in two different reactions received from two people I love dearly, Gail provided interesting comments that gave me food for thought, and Kevin expressed his pride in me for accomplishing my goal.

I want to express appreciation to my friends and family who, over the last several months, queried me on the status of the book. Their interests conveyed evidence of their faith in me, for which I am thankful.

Finally, I thank God for His guidance which helped me to tell my story.

Contents

Preface vii

Chapter One
How It All Began 1
The Gift of Prayer 5

Chapter Two
I Know You Will Help Me 7
   Background 7
   Letter 13
   Outcome 15

Psalm 121 18
The Nightingale's Praise 20

Chapter Three
Please Fix that Car, Lord, and Find Me a Buyer 22
   Background 22
   Letter 26
   Outcome 28

The Great Mystery of Life 32

Chapter Four
A Plea for Guidance and Direction in Meeting Goals 34
   Background 34
   Letter 37
   Outcome 39

Psalm 23 42
First Letter to the Reader 44

Chapter Five
Take This Cup from Me 47
    Background 47
    Letter 52
    Outcome 54

Solace 57

Chapter Six
Fear of Not Meeting Deadlines 59
    Background 59
    Letter 65
    Outcome 67

Have You Ever 70

Chapter Seven
A Plea for Help and Strength 72
    Background 72
    Letter 76
    Outcome 78

Second Letter to the Reader 82

Thanksgiving Letter 85

Chapter Eight
Reflections on the Thanksgiving Letter and on Faith 87

The Day I Spoke with Jesus 91

Psalm 100 93

Chapter Nine
Believe in Miracles! 95

Epilogue 101

Chapter One

How It All Began

I had always felt that relocating from my homeland to another country would require a lot of courage. Yet, there I was, making that decision, along with my family, and feeling somewhat scared about a permanent move to the United States. From the start, you need to know that I used to worry a whole lot. Always calm, cool, and collected on the outside, I would worry myself to death on the inside. Since I worried about every little thing, you can understand that this big move my family was contemplating was killing me slowly.

With all the tasks that had to be completed before our departure, I sometimes felt the urge to reach out to someone. However, I never did, simply because of my pride. I just did not want to share my personal struggles and problems with family or friends. Being a formal person, this was something that I could not and would not do; for me, it was just not right—end of story. So, at night, in the privacy of my bedroom, I started writing letters of prayer to the Lord. These prayers, written as letters, were very personal and simple. They conveyed exactly what my true emotions were at that time, as well as provided me with some amount of comfort. More important, they helped to tell my story as it unfolded in Jamaica and showed me that the Lord does answer our prayers.

I wrote my first letter to God shortly after my husband, Gary, left for the United States on August 3, 1984. I sought assurance from the Lord in that particular letter regarding our plans to relocate. Gary had gone ahead to pave the way for the arrival of our two children, Gail and Kevin, as well as myself, in December of that same year. From that very first letter, my habit of writing letters to the Lord took on a life of its own.

Writing letters of prayer became my regular way of communicating with the Lord. I felt so much closer to Him. It was almost as if He were sitting there with me in my bedroom, and I were talking with Him. The experience created a feeling of comfort, which inspired me to freely share everything that was within my heart. When I wrote my letters, I was no longer that proud person who did not want to share her problems with anyone. It was a truly amazing feeling, as my Lord and Savior had now become my best friend—one who loved me unconditionally and asked for nothing in return.

My days were filled with a lot of activity in getting ready to leave Jamaica. Before I settled down to write one of my letters at night, I would usually be preoccupied with the concerns of that day. As soon as I started writing, I became calmer—an effect that deepened with each stroke of my pen. This had a healing effect on my spirit; before falling asleep, I felt assured that the Lord would help me.

In spite of all this assurance and calm, my tendency to worry would surface every day. I would worry, sometimes unnecessarily, in response to every stumbling block that I encountered. The calm would only come once I knocked on the Lord's door; this happened over and over again throughout the period before my departure. I prayed often and asked the Lord to strengthen my faith in between the times that I wrote my letters. I wanted so much to stop worrying at the sign of a problem and to fully let go and let God take charge of my life.

My faith was strengthened at the end of the four-month period, and the answers to my letters of prayer were revealed. The Lord, of course, did everything in His own way, in His own time, and at His own will.

Seven Letters to Heaven was written in prayer, praise, and thanksgiving for the goodness of God and His unconditional love for me, because I felt the need to share this beautiful experience with others. The poems interspersed throughout the book were also inspired from personal incidents. I felt compelled to write "The Day I Spoke with Jesus," as the experience recounted in the poem was truly real for me. "The Nightingale's Praise" was written one Sunday morning while a nightingale warbled for about ten minutes outside my bedroom window. I found the song of that bird haunting and beautiful; it was such a precious moment in time for me that I had to immediately capture it in that poem. "The Great Mystery of Life" was done after a friend tearfully shared a personal problem with me. "Solace," "Have You Ever …" and "The Gift of Prayer" were all written in heartfelt gratitude for prayers answered.

Now walk with me on this brief journey as I share my simple story with you.

Thus, before they call I shall answer, before they stop speaking I shall have heard.

—Isaiah 65:24

* * * * *

Surely God hears our prayers. He is a merciful Father who truly loves us.

—F"T"R

* * * * *

The Gift of Prayer

The gift of prayer
Is to us
A gift of peace and of solace

The gift of prayer
Is to us
A gift of love and of blessings

The gift of prayer
Is to us
A gift of joy and of hope

No need to search for things beyond our reach
To struggle
To try to make ends meet

For every prayer is like an oasis in the desert
Providing shade and water for all to drink

Every prayer is like rain from above
Wetting the parched soil of our troubled minds

I will lift up mine eyes to the hills—from whence comes my help?

My help comes from the Lord, who made heaven and earth.

—Psalm 121:1–2

* * * * *

Chapter Two

I Know You Will Help Me

Background

August 1984 was a time in my home country when the economy was very unstable. The prices on everything had skyrocketed, and general dissatisfaction and unrest had increased among the people. The supporters of both political parties—Jamaica Labour Party (JLP) and People's National Party (PNP)—conducted protest demonstrations, and crime was rampant in the city. Some people, who could afford to, had installed burglar bars on their doors and windows. This was for protection from the burglars who roamed the streets at nights looking for access into homes.

Not a lot of money circulated in the economy, and this was noticeable from the scanty number of shoppers in stores and shopping centers. Few had money to spend on anything but food. The high prices generally of all types of goods and their scarcity were reflected in the supermarkets as well. The practice of restricting the selling of one item unless it was purchased with another item was prevalent. This was termed the "marrying of goods." One could not buy a piece of salt fish without purchasing the ackee that was needed to prepare Jamaica's famous ackee-and-salt-fish breakfast dish. Cheddar cheese, which was well known, well loved, and well used on the island, was married to the bun; you could not buy one without the other. In addition to all of this, unemployed young men stood every day on street corners and piazzas, just waiting to get into trouble.

These were some of the scenarios that planted the seed in our minds that it was perhaps time for us to relocate to the United States. An early departure from the island was ensured, as my family already had their permanent visas (also known as green cards). This, of course, certainly helped the seed to quickly germinate and reach fruition.

The idea to leave Jamaica grew by leaps and bounds as Gary and I also thought about the future of our two children, who were still young. Gail was fourteen, and Kevin was only ten years old. We constantly worried about their safety, as well as their future education. This latter concern was borne out of the fact that the University of the West Indies was the only institution of higher learning in the country at that time. To be accepted, one would need to do exceptionally well on the General Certificate of Education Examinations (GCE)—both "O" and "A" levels. This made the competition extremely high for potential students, as only a small number would be accepted each year.

A move to the United States, we believed, would definitely open a lot of doors for our children, including easier access to getting their college education. We wondered, too, if we could continue to afford living in Jamaica and whether job opportunities would be available for the children, once they completed their education. It was these additional concerns, coupled with what was happening politically in the country, which finally convinced us that we should relocate to the United States.

Gary and I had planned that he would go four months ahead of the children and me. I would remain in Jamaica, because Gail and Kevin were still in school. As a result of this decision, taking care of everything before our departure would automatically fall into my lap. We both knew that this would be quite a lot of work to be completed in four months, but it had to be done. There was not much choice at that point, as it was imperative for Gary to get things ready for us prior to our arrival in the United States, while I remained in Jamaica.

Once we had arrived at this decision, I became anxious about the problems my family would face before this big move became a reality. This was how I worried about everything! I believed I had a good enough reason to worry this time, however, as the tasks ahead seemed truly daunting. They included, among other things, selling our family car, furniture, and other household items; making arrangements to get our personal effects to the United States; preparing our home for rental; finding a tenant; settling all outstanding obligations; and getting the two children and myself ready to leave Jamaica. I felt that was quite an agenda for one person over a four-month period.

I had avoided sharing one worry in particular with my family: Deep down in my heart, I was not fully sure about leaving Jamaica.

I had an excellent job and was not convinced that I would get a similar position in the United States. The relocation, whether at that time or any other time, was something that we had to do in order to maintain our visa status, but I was just not ready to leave.

I had decided to keep these thoughts to myself because my husband and two children were so excited about living in the United States. In retrospect, my refusal to share this with them might have added to my initial stress. What made me write my first letter to God, however, was my anxiety about the preparatory work involved in the relocation, as well as some nagging questions that I had.

I spent several sleepless nights pondering these concerns. On one of those nights, as I stared in the darkness of my room, the questions rolled from one to the next. *How am I going to manage on my own over the next four months? Will I get through with everything in time for our departure? Will I have sufficient funds? Have we made the right decision to leave our homeland? Are we going to like the United States and find comparable jobs there? What about the children and drugs?* As you can see, I was truly a basket case.

Adding to all this confusion, Gary had taken with him only a meager portion of our savings—and, to make matters worse, he had no job offers. This was another nagging worry that surfaced every night.

I did not want to share these personal fears and concerns with anyone, as I knew what some people would say. *Why are you giving up your good job? Why leave this beautiful country? Why are you giving yourselves unnecessary problems? Jamaica is your homeland, and you are already established here.* "Yes," I screamed out loud in my thoughts. "Yes, this is my homeland, but I am leaving it for what I hoped would be a better life, particularly for my children!"

So, each night, I would lay in bed, wide awake and totally confused, trying to find answers to all my questions. I wanted some assurance that we had made the right decision. Most of all, I was scared—scared of the unknown. I truly begged the Lord to show me a sign before finally sitting up in bed and slowly and carefully writing my first letter to Him, which I called "I Know You Will Help Me." I folded the paper on which the letter had been written and placed it in the back of my family Bible.

And we know that all things work together for good to those who love God, to those who are the called according to His purpose.

—Romans 8:28

* * * * *

I cry out to the Lord with my voice; with my voice to the Lord I make my supplication.

I pour out my complaint before Him; I declare before Him my trouble.

—Psalm 142:1–2

* * * * *

I Know You Will Help Me

Letter

August 1984

My dear, sweet Jesus:

I am your child, and I am in need of your guidance. My problems are many, and I seek your intervention and your help.

Sweet Jesus, I am laying them at your feet tonight. I'm letting go of them and letting God take over. I will then rest in the knowledge that I am under your loving guidance and protection.

Sweet Jesus, in the same way that you clothe and feed the birds of the air, I know you will help me in this, my hour of need. Lord, you know my life; you know my suffering; you know my confusion and fears; you know all my problems. Give me strength and guidance tonight, Lord.

Jesus, you have never failed me in the past when I reached out to you. Please help me again.

The Lord is my strength and my shield; my heart trusted in Him, and I am helped; therefore my heart greatly rejoices, and with my song I will praise Him.

—Psalm 28:7

* * * * *

If you have faith and believe that there is a God, many mountains will be moved from life's troubled pathways.

—F"T"R

* * * * *

I Know You Will Help Me

Outcome

I awoke the next morning still feeling somewhat troubled. If only I could get some kind of sign that would somehow convince me that this step my family was taking was the right one. I got cold feet just thinking about leaving my homeland. One has to be really certain when planning to move from one's country to another. That certainty was what I lacked.

I was the only one in my family who still had some misgivings about leaving Jamaica. The children were overly excited about going. We had been traveling between Jamaica and the United States over the past three years, in order to not lose our visa status. These trips included lots of shopping, sightseeing, and visiting our relatives in Rochester, New York; the visits were constant vacations for my children. After all, visiting was quite different from actually living in the country and being caught up with the challenges of daily life. My children could not wait to leave. You know how young siblings usually get along close to the time of celebrations—birthdays or Christmas Eve—in anticipation of opening gifts and having fun? Well, my two were no longer fighting and were best friends as they eagerly awaited our departure. Gary, on the other hand, wanted to leave Jamaica because he felt that there would be better employment opportunities in the United States. This definitely made me singular with regards to our decision.

I read the letter I had written the night before and placed it again in my Bible. I reached over and turned on the small radio by my bedside. It was tuned to RJR—one of the island's two radio stations at the time. As the radio crackled to life, I heard, "… and so my brothers and sisters, do not be afraid to make important decisions in your lives. God will always guide you, but you will have to trust in Him and have faith. Amen." It was Sunday, and I seemed to have caught the end of a church service broadcast. I quickly turned up the volume of the radio, but was greeted with strains of "The Old Rugged Cross"—one of my favorite hymns. For a moment, I wondered if I had heard what I thought I heard. As it dawned on me that I had heard right, I just started smiling. I thought it was so wonderful that I had asked for guidance, and the response came to me through a radio program. I knew then in my heart that Gary and I had made the right decision. God surely works in a mysterious way, His wonders to perform.

I got down on my knees and said a silent prayer of thanksgiving. I asked the Lord to be ever at my side and to hold my hands in His. My prayers also included a request for Him to show me the way—not only over the next four months, but when my children and I joined my husband in the United States.

Happy is the man who finds wisdom, and the man who gains understanding; …

—Proverbs 3:13

* * * * *

In order for the Lord to help us, we need to have faith; open our minds and hearts to Him; and listen to that small voice from within.

—F"T"R

* * * * *

Psalm 121

I will lift up my eyes to the hills—
From whence comes my help?

My help comes from the Lord,
Who made heaven and earth.

He will not allow your foot to be moved;
He who keeps you will not slumber.

Behold, He who keeps Israel
Shall neither slumber nor sleep.

The Lord is your keeper;
The Lord is your shade at your right hand.
The sun shall not strike you by day,
Nor the moon by night.

The Lord shall preserve you from all evil;
He shall preserve your soul.
The Lord shall preserve your going out and your coming in
From this time forth, and even forevermore.

"Look at the birds of the air, for they neither sow nor reap nor gather into barns; yet your heavenly Father feeds them. Are you not of more value than they? ..."

—Matthew 6:26

* * * * *

There is such beauty and wonder in God's creation. Have you ever heard a bird singing off-key? The sun, the moon, the stars, and the seasons—they work with such precision that it is awesome to comprehend.

—F"T"R

* * * * *

The Nightingale's Praise

I heard the song of a nightingale
One Sunday morn as I sat in quiet repose
It sang as if it were singing a hymn of praise:
All things bright and beautiful
All creatures great and small

It sang sweetly
It stopped and looked at the world
It sang distinctly and clearly—
Many tunes depicting many moods

It sang proudly
It sang self-assuredly
It sang alone, surprisingly
As if no other bird could equal those melodies

It sang loudly
It sang hauntingly:
Glory to God on high, and on earth
Peace toward all men

The Lord is my rock and my fortress and my
deliverer; my God, my strength, in whom I will
trust; my shield and the horn of my salvation, my
stronghold.

—Psalm 18:2

* * * * *

Believe! Once you do, you will be provided with
the key to the door of many possibilities.

—F"T"R

* * * * *

Chapter Three

Please Fix that Car, Lord, and Find Me a Buyer

Background

One of the first things I had to do in my family's move to the United States was to sell our family car. I knew that it would realize a good price, and the Lord knew I needed the money. I would miss using the car, but it was probably the only piece of property we had that would generate a sizable sum of money. We had purchased it one year earlier, and although it was a used car, the previous owner had kept it in good condition. It was a nice, bright orange Lada sedan with leather interior. We were proud to own that car, and I was not too happy to part with it. However, just when I was ready to put it up for sale, it developed a problem of overheating. I had thought that this was such bad timing, since we never had any problems with the car before.

I had loaned the car to my brother-in-law, Tony, for a day, and he complained about the car overheating when he returned it to me later that evening. As he handed the keys to me I had muttered that this was just my luck, and really wondered how I was going to sell a car that was giving problem. That night I wrote my second letter titled, "Please Fix that Car, Lord, and Find Me a Buyer," and waited patiently for God's intervention.

While I waited, I ignored the problem and hoped that it was not anything too serious, and that it would somehow go away. The problem did not go away, and every day, I would fear for my life as I drove to and from work. The front of the car would become very hot after the car was driven for a few miles. At times, I felt as if I had my feet in an oven. A co-worker traveled with me to the office one morning and complained of the heat in the car. She said to me, "Girl, you are crazy driving the car in this condition. Why don't you get it fixed?" I quickly told her that I planned to have it checked. I did not want to tell her the truth: I was scared that it might be a major job, which I would not be able to handle financially.

I really hoped to take the car into the garage operated by George, our car mechanic of many years. There were several of these garages, as they were called, around town; they were used not only to store cars, but to repair them as well. George had his car-repair shop in the back of his yard. Although I passed his garage every day on my way to and from work, I kept putting off going to see him, because I just did not have the money at that time to repair the car. I had prayed for the good Lord to help me and, at the same time, I was pushing my luck with the hope that the car would not break down on the road before I came up with some money to fix it.

I worried daily about this happening, but sometimes you do what is necessary when you have no other option. So, each morning, I said a silent prayer to the Lord and drove the car to the office, and I did the same thing when I left for home in the afternoons.

In spite of the fact that the car had a heating problem, it was crucial for me to sell it as quickly as possible. I was relying on the money from the sale to take care of any financial shortfall and to settle some outstanding bills before departing from Jamaica. My predicament was so painfully obvious to me. I did not have the funds to repair the car; yet, at the same time, I needed to sell it. I also worried about not getting a buyer for the car due to the fact that the engine was overheating.

After driving the car in this condition for a week, my faith began to waver. I was sure that the Lord heard my prayer, but I was not able to come up with the funds to repair the car. I re-read the next letter—the one that I had written the night Tony returned the car to me—and I prayed once again for the Lord's help and guidance.

"Therefore do not worry about tomorrow, for tomorrow will worry about its own things. Sufficient for the day is its own trouble. …"

—Matthew 6:34

* * * * *

Why do we continue to worry about worldly objects? When we depart from this world, we leave everything behind. In our human weakness, we sometimes forget this truism and put too much focus on our possessions.

—F"T"R

* * * * *

Please Fix that Car, Lord, and Find Me a Buyer

Letter

September 1984

Sweet Jesus:

More problems. I am asking for divine order in my life and affairs.

I got back the car tonight from Tony, but Lord it was so hot—a lot of heat in the front. I hope nothing serious is wrong. Dear Lord, I need to sell that car, and I need a buyer soon. Please, God, don't let anything go wrong with that car, not now, please; and when it is bought, could you please give the buyer several months of good service from that car.

Lord, I hope that I'm not asking for too much. It is a worldly object, but I need to dispose of it in order to organize the rest of my goal(s) in December.

Sweet Jesus, I am afraid—afraid of the next two months and all that I have to do. Please, Jesus, give me strength, your kind assistance, and your guidance.

But as it is written:

"Eye has not seen, nor ear heard,
Nor have entered into the heart of man
The things which God has
prepared for those who love him."
                                        —1 Corinthians 2:9

                        * * * * *

We should all try to live one day at a time and not
worry too much about our tomorrows; because our
God is all knowing, all giving, and all caring.
                                        —F"T"R

                        * * * * *

Please Fix that Car, Lord, and Find Me a Buyer

Outcome

I continued to drive the car to work and back home for another week. I knew it would be okay to drive it for only short distances, as long as the engine was allowed to cool down. I, therefore, made sure that I only used the car when it was absolutely necessary, and I continued to pray each night.

Two weeks after writing my letter, on my drive home from work one afternoon, the Lada suddenly stopped overheating! I remember it happening while I was traveling on one of the side streets parallel to the Half-Way-Tree intersection—one of the busiest intersections in the city—which was only a few blocks from my home. The intense heat in the front of the car that I had grown accustomed to was actually no longer there. At first, it was hard to comprehend that the car that had been giving trouble for two weeks had just suddenly stopped overheating. With growing awareness, though, I realized that the Lord was simply protecting and loving me. He once again had come to my aid and had responded to my letter. He had not forgotten me, but did things in His own time. I truly felt blessed and, with tears in my eyes, said a silent prayer of thanks.

On discovering that the car was no longer overheating, I wasted no time in putting a classified advertisement in the local newspaper for the upcoming weekend. The day after the advertisement appeared in the newspaper, two interested buyers called me.

At this time, I would like to share something interesting that had happened. About eight months earlier, someone had stolen the car's tires; Gary and I awoke one morning to find the car sitting on four concrete blocks! Someone had come by our house that night and stole our rims and tires. This was not an unusual occurrence in Jamaica at the time, as the cost of living was extremely high, and acts of larceny and burglary were frequent. We were just very happy that whoever it was that had come into our yard and stolen from us had been kind enough to have left the car behind. All we had to replace were the rims and the tires.

We felt some urgency in getting this done, as we needed the car for transportation around town. The scheduling of the city buses was unreliable, so it was paramount for us to purchase the rims and tires as soon as possible and get the car back on the road.

There was only one main car dealership that had rims that would fit the car. When we got there and checked the rims, we discovered that they were the sporty and flashy types. Moreover, they were very expensive—not the kind that we would buy under normal circumstances. Unfortunately, these were not normal circumstances for us, as we urgently needed the rims, so we had no choice but to buy them.

We had not known that this was a blessing in disguise. Sometimes, without us knowing, the Lord starts putting things into place long before our needs arise—even before we turn to Him for help. What my husband and I did know, however, was that those rims made our little Lada quite attractive. I guess it was because of the unusual, yet smart-looking combination—those special rims on a bright orange Lada.

Well, it was those very sporty rims that heightened the interest of one of the two prospective buyers who had contacted me. He was a young man in his thirties, and he bought the car the very same day he laid eyes on it. The reason he gave me for purchasing it immediately was that he feared if he did not do so, it would not be there the next day, simply because of the rims. God really does work miracles, and they should be seen as such, not as mere coincidences.

I was thankful that the Lord responded to my prayers when I asked Him for help with the repair as well as the sale of my car. I felt both happy and blessed as I checked off those two items from my to-do list.

It is good that one should hope and wait quietly
for the salvation of the Lord.

—Lamentations 3:26

* * * * *

You may be broken in mind and spirit, and life
may seem hopeless and unfair. But as long as you
have the breath of life within you, there is hope
for a better tomorrow. So, look outward; reach
upward to God; and keep praying and smiling.

—F"T"R

* * * * *

The Great Mystery of Life

Life—with all its
Pain, love, trials, and happiness
What is it all about?
I think about birth, and I think about death
I think about sickness and about health
And ask, what is this mystery of life?

Why are we put here?
To be happy and then sad?
To have troubles, be burdened?
To live a good life?
To live a bad life?
What exactly is this mystery of life?

I think about suffering, pain, and poverty
I think about riches, happiness, and joy
I ask, why are evil deeds allowed to
Co-exist with good deeds?
Why do we hunger and thirst?
And in my mind's eyes I see that life is

Happiness versus sorrow
Good versus bad
Peace versus war
Equality versus inequality
All culminating in
Heaven versus hell

While He was still speaking, someone came from the ruler of the synagogue's house, saying to him, "Your daughter is dead. Do not trouble the Teacher."

But when Jesus heard it, He answered him, saying, "Do not be afraid; only believe, and she will be made well."

—Luke 8:49–50

* * * * *

We should learn to have child-like trust in God; one that is steadfast and unwavering.

—F"T"R

* * * * *

Chapter Four

A Plea for Guidance and Direction in Meeting Goals

Background

After the sale of the car, my thoughts turned next to the task of renting our home and selling our furniture.

When I looked at all the furniture Gary and I had accumulated over fifteen years of marriage, I felt sad at the thought of selling any of it. I thought about my mahogany three-piece sofa set, upholstered in beautiful green velvet, which we had bought only a year ago. This had always been a conversation piece in our living room, but the customs broker had recommended that we leave it behind. He said that the mahogany wood would not do well in the United States, as it would become infested with *chi-chi*. To this day, I still question my decision to take his recommendation. None of the other pieces of furniture we took with us to the United States were infested by termites. I regret that I did not insist that he include the set with the rest of our personal effects; that sofa set was very special to me. He also told me that the buffet was too heavy and would cost a fortune to send it overseas. It was then that I missed my husband; I really needed his support in all the decision-making.

The process of making the arrangements to dispose of the furniture and figuring out what to sell and what to take with us was not turning out to be easy for me. It only added to my burden, and I felt somewhat overwhelmed. While getting ready to move overseas, every change in plan or every obstacle seems huge, especially if you are doing things without much help from others. With all these unplanned changes and missing Gary, I really looked forward to pouring out my feelings in my letters as I sought help from the Lord. I found great comfort in doing this. Being alone in the quiet of my room each evening allowed me to meditate and be at peace.

I had set a deadline of December 1 to wrap up most, if not all, of the moving preparations that I had to do. As this time drew near, I reached out to the Lord in my prayers. I somehow expected some amount of difficulty with the outstanding tasks that remained. In my third letter, I asked for strength, support, and guidance from Him. As you can see from my letters, the Lord had become a real friend.

Praise the Lord, for the Lord is good; sing praises to His name, for it is pleasant.

—Psalm 135:3

* * * * *

Sometimes we fail to give thanks for blessings we receive, and simply rejoice at our own good fortune.

—F"T"R

* * * * *

A Plea for Guidance and Direction in Meeting Goals

Letter

October 1984

Dear God:

It is now October, and I am beginning to lean on you quite heavily as my burdens increase. There is no one to help me, and therefore I will be looking up to you for all kinds of assistance.

Sweet Jesus, you know my goals; you know my deadlines; you know, too, that sometimes I press the panic button too soon, especially when things don't go the way I plan them.

My needs are so material, Lord, but please shower me with strength, understanding, guidance, insight, and foresight.

God thunders marvelously with His voice. He
does great things which we cannot comprehend.

—Job 37:5

* * * * *

I called the Lord in distress; the Lord answered
me and set me in a broad place.

—Psalm 118:5

* * * * *

A Plea for Guidance and Direction in Meeting Goals

Outcome

Why I sometimes anticipated problems during that period of my life is something I cannot fully understand. This might have happened out of anxiety on my part. I was so stressed out that, in my mind, any disastrous thing that was possible could have happened. The word "worry" was truly my middle name! I now understand that faith plays an important role in our lives, especially when we open up our minds and our hearts to the Lord. We have to believe in His goodness and allow Him to guide us.

In spite of my shortcomings, the Lord did not give up on me, and He came to my rescue time after time. After writing my letter titled, "Plea for Guidance and Direction in Meeting Goals," I felt that I received divine order in my life in response to my plea.

To dispose of the furniture, I had placed another advertisement in the local newspaper—the Sunday edition of the *Daily Gleaner*. I got up quite early that particular Sunday morning and dusted and polished the furniture that I would be selling; I waited. While waiting, I said a silent prayer to the Lord that a lot of interested buyers would read my advertisement and come to our home.

The morning remained quiet for quite a while, and I continued to wait. I must admit that I started to feel uneasy and was ready to press that panic button, as no one was showing up at our door.

My uneasiness turned to worry as the morning wore on and no one knocked on our door. A little after midday, a steady stream of interested buyers came by our home. I was kept busy for the rest of the afternoon as the divine order played out in my life and the Lord kept answering my prayers. Selling our furniture was so easy. It did not require the kind of worrying that I had put myself through earlier that day.

All of the people who came into our home that Sunday afternoon left with a piece of our furniture. It was a bittersweet feeling; I was happy to see the furniture being purchased but was sad to part with the items.

I am happy to share that I sold everything that day—or almost everything. I did not find a buyer for the buffet and gave it away to someone who needed it.

In the next letter, which is the first of two letters to the readers of this book, I share some thoughts on my letters of prayer and my progress, if any, in terms of my request for a strengthened faith.

Look and see the trees and flowers in their entire splendor; the rich brown earth; the sun; the moon; the stars; and you. You, too, are a part of God's beautiful creation—a very special person in the eyes of our Savior.

—F"T"R

* * * * *

If we reach out to the Lord in faith, He will lovingly take our hands and guide us.

—F"T"R

* * * * *

Psalm 23

The Lord is my shepherd;
I shall not want.

He makes me to lie down in green pastures;
He leads me beside the still waters.

He restores my soul;
He leads me in the paths of righteousness
For His name's sake.

Yea, though I walk through the valley of the shadow of death,
I will fear no evil;
For you are with me;
Your rod and Your staff they comfort me.

You prepare a table before me in the presence of my enemies;
You anoint my head with oil;
My cup runs over.

Surely goodness and mercy shall follow me
All the days of my life;
And I will dwell in the house of the Lord forever.

"And I say to you, ask, and it will be given to you; seek, and you will find; knock, and it will be opened to you.

"For everyone who asks receives, and he who seeks finds, and to him who knocks it will be opened. …"

—Luke 11:9–10

* * * * *

Our heavenly Father's love for us is infinite. It opens the gate to untold blessings, and we should never be afraid to ask for His help.

—F"T"R

* * * * *

First Letter to the Reader

Dear Reader:

It was almost time for our departure from Jamaica, set for December 14, and I would like to share the following with you.

During the months leading up to our move, writing my letters of prayer had become important to me. I was under tremendous stress, and I looked forward to my evenings at home, when I would unburden my problems in my letters. As I shared earlier, my husband had gone ahead to the United States. I was on my own with two children, holding a full-time job and trying to wrap up a lifetime during a four-month period. My funds were also low, as I was operating with one income where there used to be two.

It was a scary period for me, but, as I drew nearer to my deadline, I drew closer to God. I must admit that at times, I felt somewhat guilty in going to Him so often with my problems. This, I am sure, really did not matter to our heavenly Father. Each time I wrote a letter, a feeling of calm mingled with excitement overtook me. I had stumbled onto something really special at a time when my life was fraught with confusion and problems. I called this special something my personal gold mine. You see, it was so easy for me to go to the Lord with my problems. To see divine order unfolding as the days wore on was truly a wonderful experience. It felt as if I had struck gold in this special gold mine—but instead of gold, I got blessings.

In spite of all this wonderful feeling, I was still fighting my own private battle. I was trying really hard to let go of my incessant worrying and to let God fully take charge of my life and my problems. I was happy and felt extremely blessed that the Lord had helped me each time that I called on Him. At the same time, I was unhappy with myself for not trusting Him enough to stop worrying on a regular basis.

So, as I continued wrapping up my affairs, I continued writing my letters, which provided me with some comfort. I also prayed for my faith to be strengthened.

"And all things, whatever you ask in prayer, believing, you will receive."

—Matthew 21:22

* * * * *

We should always remember that the good Lord answers our prayers, but in His own way.

—F"T"R

* * * * *

Chapter Five

Take This Cup from Me

Background

My faith continued to waver, as will be shown in this next situation. Also, the way in which my request would be answered would not be what I expected, as revealed in the outcome of this experience.

I got involved in what was called a pyramid scheme in my homeland. Also known as a network, it is a nonsustainable business transaction or plan that involves the exchange of money. This money is primarily accepted for enrolling other people in the plan, often without any product or service being delivered. A friend had introduced me to one of these money-contribution pyramids that had just been formed by two partners. This happened at a time when I urgently needed some funds to pay an overdue bill. As much as Gary wanted to help with these bills, he did not have the money to send to me. He had his own problems as he tried hard to have everything in place for our arrival in December.

I had welcomed the opportunity to make some extra cash without much thought, dutifully making the required contribution of $200.00 to this new plan. The plan had a total payout of around $1,000.00 to each person whose name made it to the apex of his or her pyramid. This was possible as long as each person in that pyramid enrolled at least one additional person or more. Each person would move up a step in the pyramid ladder as more people joined. By the time one's name reached the apex, that person would have collected the full amount of $1,000.00.

All of this sounded quite interesting to me, and I was consumed with the thought of getting quick and easy cash. This, coupled with my desperation at the time, completely overshadowed the risks involved in these pyramid plans. Being human, we are sometimes so weak, and we will succumb to taking risks when we find ourselves in dire straits.

My further recollection of this experience is that one day my friend took me to a meeting that was held at one of the partners' homes. The purpose of the meeting was to specifically collect the required $200.00 from the other gullible people like myself!

When we arrived at the partner's home, which was a very small building, I was amazed to see a crowd of about one hundred and twenty-five people all over the front yard and even on the sidewalk in front of the home. The strange thing was that they all stood in groups, which I guessed represented the people making up the different pyramids. I felt somewhat nervous at the sight of so many people and wondered what I had got myself into. My friend must have seen the worried look on my face, because she hugged me reassuringly and told me that everything was going to be okay. This helped me to relax, and I turned my focus once again to the crowd of people around me.

The meeting was being conducted inside the home, but I had no idea what was being said. I could not even make it to the door because of the large crowd. What I overheard outside were conversations of how some people had actually collected their $1,000.00 in an earlier pyramid and were at the meeting to rejoin the plan.

My friend collected my $200.00 and made the arrangements for me to bring someone at the next meeting. Before we parted, she told me that in a matter of a week or so, I would start receiving monies. If things went well, I would eventually collect the full amount of $1,000.00.

The pyramid that I had contributed to eventually crashed, as they often do, and most people lost their money. I was never told what happened, but I assumed that maybe some people pulled out at the last minute, or the organizers ran out of new members, which caused the pyramid to collapse. I had considered myself fortunate, since I got back my deposit and had already received an extra $200.00 from my friend. I did not make the $1,000.00, but I still came out on top. However, because of an unexpected situation that occurred, my good fortune did not last for long.

I started receiving phone calls weekly from a woman who apparently had been a contributor to the pyramid from which I received money. She would shout angrily over the phone in heavy Jamaican patois (dialect), which made her sound unintelligible to me in most of our conversations. Each time she called, she would demand her $200.00 from me, as if she had given it to me in the first place. Except for these harsh demands, I did not know much about her. My girlfriend had warned me of the risks involved in pyramid plans, and I wasted no time in reminding the woman of this. In one of these phone calls, I told her in no uncertain terms that I had no intention of giving any money to anyone.

At this point, she got quite upset, and threateningly said, "A gwine mek mi bredda come dung a yu office fi get back mi money; an' by force if him have to." When I heard this, I panicked and could clearly see the embarrassment for me if such a scene took place in my office. Having this woman's brother collecting her $200.00 from me by force was not going to be a pretty sight!

I was so scared that I immediately went to my boss for some fatherly advice, as I always valued his opinion. Unfortunately, all he did was to inquire why I had gotten myself involved in this pyramid plan, which he said was a foolish thing to have done. He added that I should have known better, being fully aware of the risks involved. My lame response to all this reprimanding was that I needed some cash in a hurry. Obviously, this was not the way I expected the conversation to have gone, as the response he gave me did not allay my fears.

That evening, when I got home, I knew exactly what I had to do. I had to turn to my Father above for help. I wrote my letter, and I asked for guidance. I specifically asked the Lord, to "please take this cup from me," meaning the impending embarrassment at my office. In my heart, I truly believed that I was not the one responsible for returning this woman's money to her. *I don't know her*, I thought. *She gave her $200.00 to the organizer of the pyramid and not me.* There I was, then, asking the Lord for help on the one hand—and yet on the other hand, I had my own feelings on the matter. These feelings certainly did not include a desire to return the money. Filled with fear and worry, I wrote the fourth letter, asking for guidance and waited for the Lord's help.

Give ear to my prayer, O God; and do not hide
Yourself from my supplication.

—Psalm 55:1

* * * * *

Hear me when I call, O God of my righteousness!
You have relieved me when I was in distress; have
mercy on me and hear my prayer.

—Psalm 4:1

* * * * *

Take This Cup from Me

Letter

November 1984

My dear Lord:

I am again seeking your kind assistance. I am afraid and need your guidance on a particular problem.

I got myself involved in this risky pyramid game, and now I am facing possible embarrassment on my job.

Sweet Jesus, you have never failed me in the past when I reach out to you. Please help me this time and save me from this embarrassment. Please take this cup from me.

Thank you, Lord.

Trust wholeheartedly in Yahweh (God), put no faith in your own perception.

Acknowledge him in every course you take, and he will see that your paths are smooth.

—Proverbs 3:5–6

* * * * *

It is not easy to continue to trust and believe when our problems don't seem to be going away. In such instances we should pray to God for enlightenment to His will and try to listen closely to the voice within.

—F"T"R

* * * * *

Take This Cup from Me

Outcome

The letter that I wrote titled, "Take This Cup from Me," was placed in the back of my Bible, where I kept all my written prayers. Needless to say, the calm that I had experienced immediately after I wrote the prayer started to diminish as my faith wavered. I now began to worry more and more each day about the situation in which I had found myself. *Where is my strengthened faith?* I thought to myself. *Why am I not letting go and letting God take care of me?* My faith was so weak. Instead of trusting God, I worried constantly about the embarrassment of this woman's brother coming to my office to demand her money from me—and by force, if necessary. Furthermore, I did not want to find out what form of action the "by force" would take.

One day, at around noon, I received a call from the telephone operator at the front desk of my office informing me that a woman was on her way up to see me. (The security is stricter now in the company where I used to work.) As this woman approached my desk, I noticed how cheaply she was dressed and that she had a weary look on her face. At that point, I did not know who she was, but I was filled with compassion for this stranger. When she introduced herself as the woman who had been calling me, I was astonished. She further told me that she worked as a maid and really needed the money to help feed her children.

After hearing her story, all the negative thoughts I had had about this woman flashed through my mind, and I felt as if they disappeared into the air. For a moment, I just stared at her, filled with a new understanding of her situation. I then calmly asked her to have a seat and told her that I would be back shortly. I did not have $200.00 at that time, but I just knew that I had to get it from someone.

I left my desk and went to see a dear friend, Millicent, who was a co-worker. She was a very kind and understanding person, and I knew that she would help me if she could. Millicent did not have sufficient cash on her to cover the amount, but she gave me a check for $200.00. I was thankful and promised to pay her back at the end of the week, when I received my paycheck.

The Lord continued working this special miracle. I quickly went to the bank, which was located in the same building as my office, and cashed the check for the $200.00. I felt blessed because it was drawn on the same bank and I did not have to go outside of the building to get the cash. When I got back to my office, I handed the money to the woman without saying a word. She looked up at me with a big, broad smile on her face and said, "Tenk yu very much, ma'am; an' God bless yu!"

Whenever I think about this experience, I still marvel at the goodness of God. Remember, now, that I had no intention of giving back any money to this woman. In my action that day, I was truly guided by the Lord. He surely took away that cup from me in His own way!

After I received this wonderful guidance from the Lord, my thoughts now focused on renting our home to a good tenant.

A man's heart plans his way, but the Lord directs his steps.

—Proverb 16:9

* * * * *

We often have our own plan in mind, but by the end of the day, we find that our life has taken on a different plan, utterly unlike the one we started out with; yet, we are better off for it.

—F"T"R

* * * * *

Solace

It is truly, truly comforting
Knowing there's someone up above
Someone full of understanding
Compassion, kindness, and love

When life becomes distressing
And our spirit is oh-so-low
We pray for strength and blessings
And answers to things we don't know

God makes our burdens seem lighter
By showing us how much He cares
Our lives become much brighter
As He takes away pain and tears

Yes, there's solace in His teachings
Spiritual food for all to partake
Reach out—His love is yours for the taking
All yours in the Lord's name's sake

But looking at them, Jesus said, "With men it is impossible, but not with God; for with God all things are possible."

—Mark 10:27

* * * * *

"If you ask anything in My name, I will do it. ..."

—John 14:14

* * * *

Chapter Six

Fear of Not Meeting Deadlines

Background

I wrote my fifth letter to God while in the midst of renting our home and moving out to stay with my in-laws. It was really a chaotic and emotional time for me. There was a constant flow of incoming bills requiring attention. It was as if the whole world knew that we were leaving Jamaica and wanted their accounts settled and closed. I had so much to do. I reached out to the Lord and told him about all my needs and concerns; at the same time, I continued to worry. Now isn't that strange? That's exactly what my weakened faith was doing to me.

Renting our home was crucial. There was no way we could afford to pay the full amount of the mortgage on our home in

Jamaica and, at the same time, pay rent in the United States. Gary and I debated long and hard as to whether or not we should try to sell our home before leaving for the United States. We agreed that we would not, so that if we ever decided to return to Jamaica to live, we would not have to worry about finding a new home. If I felt sad about parting with some of the furniture in our home, you can imagine how I felt when the time came for my children and me to move out of it.

Having to move out of our home brought the stark reality to me that we were really leaving Jamaica. The months of planning and preparation were finally coming to an end. The children were now missing their father. Our weekly telephone conversations with him were filled with details of their week without him, as he told us of his plans for our arrival on December 14. All three of us were beginning to slowly let go of our country and to focus our thoughts on what life would be like living permanently in the United States. We spoke daily of our upcoming new life with enthusiasm.

I had fully accepted our decision to relocate and was even looking forward to leaving my homeland. After all, I had received God's clearance on this, in that sign for which I had prayed. In the meantime, during all of this daydreaming, I was kept busy taking care of clearing up all personal matters in Jamaica and getting myself, as well as the children, ready for the big day. A major part of that preparation included arranging for them to be taken out of school and getting all the necessary vaccine shots taken care of before our departure. I had to coordinate with Gary as well, on the initial steps of getting them into schools in the United States. My plate was really full.

Packing boxes of small items that we were either taking with us or leaving behind was now the latest item on my agenda. The other thing that was most important was that the onus was now on me to find the right person to be a tenant in our home.

We were going to be living so far away, and I worried about finding someone whom we could trust. That was the number-one criteria. I wanted someone who would also treat our home as if it belonged to him or her. That person would need to properly maintain both the inside and outside of our home and take good care of our beautiful garden. I did not want to lose our garden. I had often looked through my kitchen window with admiration and pride at our well-kept lawn, the bougainvillea plants with pink and white flowers, and the crotons that lined our driveway. After years of care and constant watering, our crotons had finally displayed all the colors of the rainbow in their big, broad leaves. Even these I did not want to lose; I did not want them to die from lack of care. I secretly hoped whoever I got would love plants.

I now needed to prepare our home for rental, and this required some painting. It did not need a total paint job, but only to be touched up in some small areas. Again, I missed Gary and his support and wondered how good a job I would do on my own with this task. Fortunately, I did not have to buy any paint, as we had a few cans left over from the last time we painted our home.

One Saturday morning, I rolled up my sleeves and got ready to tackle the painting. I recall that while I was painting, one of my close business acquaintances, Marcia, came by our home to say good-bye. The time was drawing near for our departure, and this was a regular occurrence—friends and family visiting us to say good-bye and to wish us well. While we talked, Marcia helped me to paint the window shutters and frames on the second level of our home, which were easily accessible from the balcony. Her assistance was a welcome help, and the painting was completed earlier than I had planned.

Our home was now ready for rental, and I was encouraged to go to the Lord with my request to find a tenant when I recalled the story of my girlfriend Mary. She had had a miraculous breakthrough with a prayer request involving a tenant. Mary and her husband, James, had a small printing business, which they had been unsuccessfully trying to sell for the past five years. Because they were unable to get a buyer due to the economic situation in the country, they were forced to lease the business. Unfortunately, their problems increased, as during the last of those five years, the lessee owed twelve months of back rent.

Mary had been a long-standing member of Unity of Jamaica and had often invited me to join one of their weekly prayer sessions. She had shared with me that at the beginning of every year, the members of the congregation would write prayer requests to the Lord. These requests would be placed in self-addressed envelopes, to be held by the church for the year. After a year of prayers over the combined requests, they would be mailed out to the individual members.

In her prayer request to the Lord, Mary had asked for help with the problems she was having with her family business. She had happily updated me that on reading the letter request she had written one year earlier, she realized that her prayers had been answered. The lessee not only paid the back rent, but had actually bought the business—and at a much higher price than she and her husband had expected.

This reinforced my belief that the good Lord does answer our prayers, whether we communicate with Him by writing letters or writing prayer requests or getting down on our knees and praying.

However, He does so in His own way, at His own will, and in His own time. With renewed confidence, in my next and fifth letter titled, "Fear of Not Meeting Deadlines," I asked for the Lord's help in finding a good tenant.

Lord:

For those of us who are in despair, grant us hope. For those of us who are afraid or worried about what the future might hold, give us courage. Comfort those of us, Lord, who are in pain or otherwise need comforting. Most of all, Lord, if it is your will, please take away whatever burdens that we are carrying, which we are finding difficult to bear.

—F"T"R

* * * * *

O, give thanks to the Lord, for He is good! For
His mercy endures forever.

—Psalm 136:1

* * * * *

We can always expect unconditional love and
strength from God, who expects nothing in
return.

—F"T"R

* * * * *

Fear of Not Meeting Deadlines

Letter

November 1984

Dear Sweet Jesus:

I know that this is now becoming too much of a habit, but Lord, I have no one to turn to with all that I have to do except you, my Lord.

The time is drawing nearer, and when I think of all the things that I have to do, I find it most frightening. Lord, I'm now wondering if I'm going to get through with everything in time. I need money to do certain things. I received two calls today asking for money. Please, Lord, no more of these, and most of all, I need a good tenant for the house.

Please, Lord, help me. I'm lost and confused without your assistance.

Is anyone among you suffering? Let him pray. Is
anyone cheerful? Let him sing psalms.

—Isaiah 5:13

* * * * *

There are times when we get so caught up in our
problems and troubles that we forget to reach out
to God. We should remember that He is always
waiting on our call for help.

—F"T"R

* * * * *

Fear of Not Meeting Deadlines

Outcome

After writing my fifth letter, I am happy to share that the pieces of my life started to fall into place, like a jigsaw puzzle. Each of my requests had received an answer, but in my human weakness, I still felt nervous about the unfinished tasks. The uncanny thing was that every time I wrote a letter, I immediately felt calm. I wished, though, that this calm would remain with me at all times.

I did not have to advertise for the rental of our home as the word got around through friends and family that I was trying to find a good tenant. One thing I remember, most vividly, was that I rented our home to the first family who looked at it, because they fulfilled all my expectations. Divine guidance came into play as the Lord once again responded to my request.

At this time, I should mention that one of our neighbors, Mr. Beckford (now deceased), who was a kind gentleman, promised to assist in whatever way that he could in our absence. Specifically, he had mentioned helping with any small plumbing job that needed to be done around our home. Our blessings continued to increase as another dear friend, Allan, offered to take care of collecting the rent and depositing it in our bank account. Everything good just fell into place as my personal gold mine increased with godly blessings.

When Kevin, Gail and me finally moved out of our home, I was really pleased, because everything had gone so well. The Lord not only found me a good tenant, but He provided help in other areas that related to the renting of our home. This kind of help meant so much to Gary and me and would put our minds at ease, just knowing that our home would be in capable hands.

We sold our home in Jamaica about six years after we relocated to the United States. Unfortunately, the tenant did not stay there for the entire period, which was one of the main reasons we decided to sell at that time. I hasten to say that the Lord did respond to my call when I approached Him to find a tenant; whatever transpired afterward was just a part of His plan for us. I did not question this, but said thanks to God and accepted His will.

In my sixth letter, I continued to seek strength and more faith. I was also in need of money to attend to some personal matters, and this need was part of my next request.

But without faith it is impossible to please Him, for he who comes to God must believe that He is, and that He is a rewarder of those who diligently seek Him.

—Hebrews 11:6

* * * * *

My God, my God, here I am, sitting by your feet. You are trying to tell me not to worry. Give me the grace that I need to make my faith firm.

—F"T"R

* * * * *

Have You Ever ...

Have you ever thought of life's many problems?
Felt that worrying was quite unnecessary
As life was just a one-way street?

Have you ever felt a certain calm?
Let go of all your troubled thoughts?

Have you ever pretended all was well?
Drifted off in a state of unreal bliss?
Experienced an inner strength?

Well, I have had all of those feelings
They're truly very special feelings

Feelings projected from a strong faith
Feelings that have provided solace
Feelings that come from knowing I'm a child of God

Yes, I have tapped into my own gold mine
A gold mine that replaces despair with hope

A never-ending source of strength
That transforms fear into courage
And provides comfort when it is needed

I've realized that I'm only one sheep of the great flock
All equally cared for by the good and loving Shepherd
And that there are some things only He alone can change

If any of you lacks wisdom, let him ask of God, who gives to all liberally and without reproach, and it will be given to him.

But let him ask in faith, with no doubting, for he who doubts is like a wave of the sea driven and tossed by the wind.

—James 1:5–6

* * * * *

Whenever we pray for help, we should start by believing that the good Lord will hear and answer our prayers.

—F"T"R

* * * * *

Chapter Seven

A Plea for Help and Strength

Background

Our departure was now only a couple of weeks away. After months of preparing for this event, I realized that taking care of everything on my own was really not easy, and I missed Gary's companionship and support. It was a good thing that we had moved in with my in-laws. Living with them, albeit for a short period, provided lots of special, happy, and memorable occasions. Gail and Kevin thoroughly enjoyed the opportunity of spending some extra quality time with their grandparents before leaving; and I was able to give my full attention to the last few items on my to-do list.

One of my top priorities had been to settle all our accounts. There was not much of a choice for Gary and me in this matter;

our creditors expected full payment and closure of all accounts before we left Jamaica. Having to take care of this, however, and everything else relating to our move, had almost depleted our savings.

Coupled with this, although I continued with my regular prayers to the Lord and thanked Him for His many blessings, I really started feeling guilty of writing a letter of prayer almost exclusively when I was faced with a problem—not when I was happy or thankful. I believe the reason for this is that the good Lord was answering my prayers, and it all seemed so easy—me making the requests through my letters and receiving all those blessings. In retrospect, I am sure God understood and was happy to hear from me each time I reached out to Him for help. I knew that He was not keeping tabs on how many times I prayed to Him through these letters or when or why I wrote them; nor was He holding any grudges or settling any scores. He was just there to shower me with His love, which is available to all. It is that simple.

I guess that was all I needed to know, so I was truly specific in my next request for the funds I needed to help meet my final financial obligation, and also to get the children and myself ready for our departure mid-December. I would like to add here that the Lord gave me strength to face my problems each time I prayed for it, but as usual, I would initially worry when faced with another crisis. I wanted so much for this God-given strength to remain with me, but in my human weakness, I would just start fretting again at the least sign of a problem. At times, I felt that I was truly letting go of worrying about my problems, but old habits do not go away so easily. It was a slow process, but I knew in my heart that one day, I would have my faith fully strengthened, and then I would stop worrying so much.

Why are we so weak sometimes instead of trusting God? I guess it is not easy to let go of our problems and leave them in our Lord's hands. In order to do this, one need to pray continually for unwavering faith, as well as guidance and patience.

I continued to pray for all three—a stronger faith, guidance, and patience—in the sixth of my letters.

I love the Lord, because He has heard my voice
and my supplications.

Because He has inclined His ear to me, therefore
I will call upon Him as long as I live.

—Psalm 116:1–2

* * * * *

Now this is the confidence that we have in Him,
that if we ask anything according to His will, He
hears us.

—1 John 5:14

* * * * *

A Plea for Help and Strength

Letter

(Early) December 1984

Dear Jesus:

I've been putting off approaching you in this manner, as I find that I come to you mostly when I need something. This happens only because I'm weak, Lord.

Now, I've become desperate, as my funds are extremely low. I know that you have come to my assistance and aid so many, many times in the past. Lord, for this, I humbly tell you how thankful I am for your great mercy!

You once said, "Ask, and it shall be given you; seek and ye shall find; knock and it shall be opened unto you." Lord, I'm now knocking at your door, seeking your kind and merciful intervention in my life.

Also, Lord, I know that I should be patient and await your direction. I also know that you are looking after my welfare, but you know, Lord, that I'm weak, scared, and worried. Most of all, Lord, you know that I am human and subject to human frailties.

Please, Lord, give me the strength to be patient and calm while I await your instructions and directions. Give me more faith, Lord, in this hour of need.

Thank you, Lord, for everything.

Blessed be the Lord, who daily loads us with benefits, the God of our salvation! Selah.

—Psalm 68:19

* * * * *

If we do not immediately receive a response to our prayer, this does not mean that the Lord is not listening. Sometimes He chooses not to answer our request because He has something else in mind for us.

—F"T"R

* * * * *

A Plea for Help and Strength

Outcome

Just reaching out to the Lord in "A Plea for Help and Strength" calmed my fears, and as usual, I felt at peace. I continued to pray for this peace to remain with me—that my faith would not waver again under the pressure of my problems.

Four days after writing this letter, I went to visit one of my very good friends. I had known this friend for many years and really felt comfortable in her presence and in her home. We sat for a while on her verandah and discussed how goods and services were so expensive, and talked about the political situation in the country, as well as the high crime rate, especially in Kingston. Our conversation then turned from mundane stuff to more personal issues, as my girlfriend inquired about the well-being of the children. Through sips of iced-cold lemonade served in bright red glasses, we swapped stories of our children—my two and her daughter—and shared information on church activities and our jobs.

During our conversation, I was pleasantly distracted by the beauty of that bright, sunny day set against a backdrop of the majestic Blue Mountains in the distance. I took a mental snapshot of this scenery to add to my special memories of Jamaica for reflection during the cold winter months in the United States. My memory bank now had in store two such unique snapshots, including one saved earlier when I took Gail and Kevin to see our last movie at the drive-in theater at Harbour View. That night, there was a full moon, which cast a beautiful golden pathway on the waters of the Kingston Harbour. I was quickly brought out of my reverie by my girlfriend's voice when she asked, "So, Terry, how are you managing without Gary?"

Being the proud person that I am, my initial reaction was to smile sweetly and tell her everything was just fine. However, a small voice within me said, "Be honest; you never know where this will lead."

I still hesitated, and she again asked if I was sure that everything was all right. With eyes brimming with tears, I shared with her my current financial problem. She took my hands in hers and told me that she had wanted to offer some assistance, but she knew I was very proud, and she did not know how to bring up the subject. She then begged me to allow her to help. I immediately told her that I did not want to burden or bother her with my problems and that I would be okay. My girlfriend did not let up, and told me that she, too, had a similar problem in the past and fully understood my situation. She added that we were all here on this earth to help each other. Before I left for home that day, my dearest friend gave me an interest-free loan with the condition that it could be repaid at any time. I was completely astonished by this added blessing and demonstration of love and kindness.

A couple of days earlier, I had needed some funds and had prayed about it. I then received help from someone who had been watching from a distance and knew my plight. I really believe that my girlfriend had received some guidance from above. God knew that I would not have raised this issue of money myself. He opened the door, however, in His own way, which allowed her to do some gentle prodding in order that my prayer could be answered.

This experience brought to mind the story of a nurse, fondly known as Ms. Vie, who lost her sight when she was in her late-thirties. Many prayers were offered on her behalf, that one day she would see again, and she also had her own hopes of this happening. She never regained her sight, but lived an exemplary and selfless life. She helped others in a loving, kind, and supportive way, including her family and the staff of the hospital where she continued to work until her retirement. Ms. Vie passed away several years ago, and I believe that she will be remembered as someone who was unselfish, and had a positive outlook on life in spite of her challenges. God had chosen to answer those prayers offered on her behalf quite differently than the way He answered mine, but nevertheless He had answered them in His own way.

The Lord's answer to the request made in my sixth letter was perfectly timed, as it coincided with our departure date—which was only days away. My next and last of two letters to the readers addresses the final leg of my journey.

The righteous cry out, and the Lord hears, and delivers them out of all their troubles.

—Psalm 34:17

* * * * *

Wait on the Lord;
Be of good courage,
And He shall strengthen your heart;
Wait, I say, on the Lord!

—Psalm 27:14

* * * * *

Second Letter to the Reader

Dear Reader:

The day finally came for Gail, Kevin, and me to leave the sunny shores of our homeland for a new life in the United States. Did I feel nervous? My answer was a resounding no! Were there any uncertainties? Not as many as I had in the first few months of my planning. The few that remained bordered on the question as to whether I would, personally, like living in this country where we were bound.

After those past months of communicating with the Lord through my letters, I felt calm and at ease. I noticed that this feeling did not leave me, but remained with me. I had finally come to a place where my faith was so much stronger than it had been before. You may wonder about this, since I was always worrying about every little thing, instead of trusting in the goodness of God. All I can say is that I came to the realization that He truly cared for me and, most important, He cared for me at all times—not only when I went to Him in prayers.

He had done so much for me. He answered my prayers each time that I called out to Him. He had walked with me as a close friend during my months of preparation. He was there during the times when I was filled with confusion and doubts. He filled my coffers when I was short of money. Most of all, He comforted me when I was afraid by calming my fears. He never really left my side; even during the times when I worried about everything. What I realized and came to believe was that I seemed to have lived right into having my faith strengthened! This had not happened overnight, but gradually. It was only at the end of my four-month journey that I finally got it: there had been absolutely no reason for me to worry about everything. The good Lord had been doing just that for me!

So, with my strengthened faith, I was even more convinced that the Lord walked with me and my children as we boarded that Air Jamaica plane, which took us to a new life in the United States of America.

Dear Reader, I will say no more at this time, except to share that my strengthened faith in God made me whole and to ask you to continue walking with me on this journey. My seventh letter reveals my thankfulness for all of God's goodness.

I sought the Lord, and He heard me, and delivered me from all my fears.

—Psalm 34:4

* * * * *

I have called upon You, for You will hear me, O God; incline Your ear to me, and hear my speech.

Show Your marvelous lovingkindness by Your right hand, O You who save those who trust in You from those who rise up against them.

Keep me as the apple of Your eye; hide me under the shadow of Your wings, …

—Psalm 17:6-8

* * * * *

Thanksgiving Letter

February 1985 (Maryland, USA)

Dear Lord:

The same way that I come to you for help, Sweet Jesus, I'm coming to you in praise.

You have been extremely kind and good to me in the past and even more recently. You continue to respond to my prayers and to show me that you are real: a good shepherd, a Good Samaritan, a tower of strength, a beacon in the dark, a caring savior, a pair of outstretched hands in times of distress, a constant friend, a companion, and, indeed, the redeemer of mankind.

Dear Lord, help me to seek you more often, and not only in times of distress and problems.

I thank you, Lord, for everything—both great and small.

Amen and amen.

Then He said to the woman, "Your faith has saved you. Go in peace."

—Luke 7:50

* * * * *

Chapter Eight

Reflections on the Thanksgiving Letter and on Faith

I specifically wanted my seventh and final letter, which I titled, "Thanksgiving Letter," to clearly show the gratitude that I felt for all that the Lord had done for me and continues to do. After reviewing my letters of prayer, I could clearly see the help, guidance, and spiritual support I received from the Lord. This compelled me to express my humble gratitude in that simple and special prayer of thanksgiving to Him. I did not want to ask the Lord for anything this time around; I wanted only to express my thankfulness. In spite of this, I did make a small request. I asked the Lord in this prayer to help me to seek Him more often and not only in times of distress. The reason for this request is that each of the letters in *Seven Letters to Heaven*, with the exception of the one titled, "Thanksgiving Letter," was written whenever I experienced a problem. This is true, as my story took place at a time in my life when I was faced with a lot of problems.

I still believe that it takes some amount of courage to move from one country to another. I must admit that during those few months, I lacked the courage to move forward boldly in some situations without worrying. In order to reinforce the requests made in my letters, I also prayed to the Lord verbally for His help in all my circumstances. Writing my letters, therefore, was one way of praying that I used when the going got especially tough. I continued to pray to the Lord, as usual, each night and day.

It has been twenty-five years since my family left Jamaica, and I still write letters of prayer, mostly when I feel deeply troubled about something. It really makes me feel so much closer to God. I also continue to express my gratitude for God's unconditional love and guidance—verbally and in written prayers of thanksgiving.

I know that some people may be skeptical that one could reasonably expect to receive an answer to a prayer by simply writing a letter. My initial response to this would be that it is quite easy to use a letter as a form of prayer to seek guidance from God. Furthermore, when you are not sure how to pray or what to say, writing is an easier way to convey, more clearly, your thoughts and requests. Receiving an answer to your request, however, requires a lot of faith and trust in the Lord.

I am referring to the kind of faith that will make you pass your request to God with confidence and trust, and believing with all your heart that He will take charge of the situation or provide an answer. It is the kind of faith that will not waver when you have a problem, because you just know that God will take care of you. This is the lesson that I learned after that four-month period in Jamaica: the lesson that there is no need to worry, because God will always take care of me. I now believe this with all my heart; this is how my faith was finally strengthened.

Here is another thought that I would like to share with you: I think of myself as very special in God's eyes. This is a powerful and confident statement, and I would like you to bear with me as I further explain it. I also know that no one can take this feeling away from me, as I own it! I sincerely hope that there are others who also feel this way because we are *all* God's children—each and every one of us. Moreover, we are all entitled to feel this way, but we have to, individually, own that feeling and believe it too! It is that simple. God is always in the background, looking out for our interests and needs. He loves all of us and wants so much to be a part of our lives. He wants to help us, but we have to trust and have faith in Him.

My life today and who I am reflects this renewed faith, which is now solid as a rock. Additionally, whenever I feel the need to write a letter of prayer, I now do so without being specific about what I want or what I need. I simply pass the problem or concern over to God and ask Him for His kind intervention, guidance, and direction in my life, in whatever way He sees fit!

The Lord continues to look after me and hold my hands. He has actually been doing this ever since I asked Him in that prayer request made shortly after He answered my very first letter. I have also come to realize that during this journey called life, we all stumble and fall for various reasons. We should never forget that the Lord is always there to catch us, if we will only reach out to Him.

I have now finally reached the end of my brief journey with you, and I will next share why I believe in writing letters of prayer and in miracles.

If you have faith and truly believe in the Almighty, you will find answers even in the wind whispering through the trees as it gently soothes and calms your troubled mind.

—F"T"R

* * * * *

Try to let go and let God take care of your life. Make it a habit of trusting the Lord and you will be filled with an inner strength and peace.

—F"T"R

* * * * *

The Day I Spoke with Jesus

I reached out to Him one day
With trembling hands and tear-filled eyes
I reached out to Him one day
Because I needed someone who cared
Someone who would listen
Someone who would make my shaken world right

I spoke out loudly to Him in my misery
And a miracle unfolded
He spoke back within my heart with compassion
With complete joy in my heart, I spoke again
He answered with great love and a voice so gentle
My child, be still, and wait

I waited and it happened
His love, strength, and guidance were manifested
He made my problems seem light
He gave me the will to fight
He replaced my weakness with strength and wisdom
He showed me the way that I could reach out to Him

I know that I've found a real friend in Jesus
I reach out to Him every day of my life
And, yes, oh yes, He is always there
I know that I'm very special in His eyes, and so are you
You, too, can share in this wonderful experience
With strong and unwavering faith
And a belief in miracles

You will show me the path of life; in Your presence is fullness of joy; at Your right hand are pleasures forevermore.

—Psalm 16:11

* * * * *

Prayers help to heal and often fill a spiritual void in our lives.

—F"T"R

* * * * *

Psalm 100

Make a joyful shout to the Lord, all you lands!

Serve the Lord with gladness;
Come before His presence with singing.

Know that the Lord He is God;
It is He who has made us, and not we ourselves;
We are His people and the sheep of His pasture.

Enter into His gates with thanksgiving,
And into His courts with praise.
Be thankful to Him, and bless His name.

For the Lord is good;
His mercy is everlasting,
And His truth endures to all generations.

Ingredients for Putting a Little Sunshine Back in
Your Life

- Try sometimes to see the world like a child—no
  care, no worry
- Take time to gaze in awe and wonder at a starry
  sky and enjoy its beauty
- On a rainy day, look heavenward and let the rain
  fall on your face
- Most of all, believe in miracles

—F"T"R

* * * * *

Chapter Nine

Believe in Miracles!

Yes, the Lord told me, "My child, be still and wait." Well, as you can see, I wrote my letters of prayer, and I waited. I was able to finalize all outstanding matters—with the help and guidance of my special friend, who was always there for me and still is.

I joined my husband in the United States on December 14, 1984, along with our two children. He knew that things had not been easy for me with him being away, especially in terms of our finances. My ears were filled with his expressions of how really proud he was of me and how much he regretted that he had not been there physically to help and support me. He was amazed that I had accomplished so much and had done so well without help from anyone. He was fully aware that I had sold the car that was giving us trouble; disposed of most of the furniture that we had accumulated over the years; tied up all loose ends; paid all our outstanding bills and other obligations; and finally, rented our home, among other things.

What my husband did not know was that everything had gone smoothly, and I had met all my goals, only with God's help. I also needed to share with him my realization that the good Lord was always with me and was always ready to move all the mountains in my pathway. It was important for me to also tell him how my faith was strengthened and that, finally, I had stopped worrying incessantly. Most of all, I wanted him to know that I truly believe in miracles because of what had transpired during those last four months in Jamaica.

So, if ever you feel the need to talk to someone, to unload a burden, to find answers to some of life's problems, or only to give thanks, remember that there is a personal friend above. Try writing Him a letter of prayer. In times of need, spiritual or otherwise, sit quietly and write a letter to the Lord. Try to tell Him what is hurting you or causing you to worry. Tell Him what is on your mind and share with Him your heartaches and your joys. The simple act of putting your thoughts on paper will help to alleviate some of the stress you may be going through.

Write as many letters to God as you wish—the Lord will never get tired of hearing from you. You will also feel a sense of relief once you have written out your problems or concerns. This sense of relief will come from the fact that you have shared what is bothering you with someone who can make things right—one who truly loves you.

Your letters could also serve as a wonderful reminder of your interaction with God. You could always look back at some of them whenever your spirit needs uplifting. You may even be amazed and surprised at the outcome, if someday in the future you decide to compare your letters of prayer with the events that have transpired in your life.

It is important, however, for you to have unwavering faith and to believe that with God, all things are possible. The Bible reveals this truth time and time again. To be receptive of His guidance and goodness, though, you will need to open your mind and heart to Him. Only then will you discover that you have tapped into a gold mine of blessings that is free to everyone.

It has been a joy to be able to share my experience with others. I am thankful to those readers who took this brief walk with me to that special place that I stumbled upon through my letters of prayer. It is a place of very strong faith that has brought me closer to God, made Him a special friend, and brought me solace in times of need. I have, indeed, found *my* personal gold mine, filled with a lot of blessings. Furthermore, I feel particularly blessed that I continue to receive positive direction and guidance in my life through answered prayers. With regards to unanswered prayers, I accept the Lord's will, knowing that the response will be revealed in His own time, in His own way, and at His own will.

Finally, I hope that sharing my story has fulfilled its purpose, which has been to provide encouragement and inspiration to others. Also, never stop believing in miracles!

> Be anxious for nothing, but in everything by prayer and supplication, with thanksgiving, let your requests be made known to God;
>
> and the peace of God, which surpasses all understanding, will guard your hearts and minds through Christ Jesus.
>
> —Philippians 4:6–7

So Jesus answered and said to them, "Have faith in God.

"For assuredly, I say to you, whoever says to this mountain, 'Be removed and be cast into the sea,' and does not doubt in his heart, but believes that those things he says will come to pass, he will have whatever he says.

"Therefore I say to you, whatever things you ask when you pray, believe that you receive them, and you will have them. ..."

—Mark 11:22–24

* * * * *

The beauty of the rainbow after a storm heralds a bright, new beginning filled with hope and promise.

—F"T"R

* * * * *

Epilogue

I n the following pages are copies of the seven original letters on which my story was based; written during the period of August 1984–December 1984, in Jamaica, with the exception of the "Thanksgiving Letter," which was written in Maryland, USA. This latter prayer was written a couple of months after our arrival.

The seven letters are listed below under their respective titles and in the order that they appear in the book.

- "I Know You Will Help Me," August 1984: Page 13
- "Please Fix that Car, Lord, and Find Me a Buyer," September 1984: Page 26
- "A Plea for Guidance and Direction in Meeting Goals," October 1984: Page 37
- "Take This Cup from Me," November 1984: Page 52
- "Fear of Not Meeting Deadlines," November 1984: Page 65
- "A Plea for Help and Strength," December 1984: Page 76
- "Thanksgiving Letter," February 1985: Page 85

August 1984

My dear sweet Jesus:

I am your child, and I am in need of your guidance. My problems are many, and I seek your intervention and your help.

Sweet Jesus, I am laying them at your feet tonight. I'm letting go of them and letting God take over. I will then rest in the knowledge that I am under your loving guidance and protection.

Sweet Jesus, in the same way that you clothe and feed the birds of the air, I KNOW YOU WILL HELP ME IN THIS, my HOUR OF NEED. Lord, you know my life; you know my suffering; you know my confusion and fear; you know ALL my problems. Give me strength and guidance tonight, Lord.

Jesus, you have never failed me in the past when I reached out to you. Please help me again!

"I Know You Will Help Me"—letter dated August 1984

September 1984

Dear Jesus:

More problems. I am asking for Divine Order in my life and affairs.

I got back the car tonight from Tony but Lord it was so hot — a lot of heat in the front. I hope nothing serious is wrong. Dear Lord, I need to sell that car and I need a new one soon. Please God don't let anything go wrong with that car, no pay?, please; and when it is bought, could you please give the buyer several months of good service from that car.

Lord, I hope that I'm not asking for too much — it is a worldly object, but I need to dispose of it in order to organize the rest of my goal(s) in December.

Dear Jesus, I AM AFRAID — afraid of the need mostly and all that I have to do. Please, Jesus, give me STRENGTH, YOUR KIND ASSISTANCE AND YOUR GUIDANCE.

"Please Fix that Car, Lord, and Find Me a Buyer"
—letter dated September 1984

October 1984

Dear God:

It is now October, and I am beginning to lean on you quite heavily as my burdens increase. There is no one to help me and, therefore, I will be looking up to you for all kinds of assistance.

Sweet Jesus, you know my goals; you know my deadline; you know, too, that I sometimes press the panic button too soon, especially when things don't go the way I plan them.

My needs are so material, Lord, but please shower me with strength, understanding, guidance, insight and foresight.

"A Plea for Guidance and Direction in Meeting Goals"
—letter dated October 1984

November 1984

My dear Lord:
I am again seeking your kind assistance. I am afraid and need your guidance on a particular problem.
I got myself involved in this risky pyramid game, and now I am facing possible embarrassment on my job.
Sweet Jesus, you have never failed me in the past when I reach out to you. Please help me this time and save me from the embarrassment.
Please take this cup from me.

Thank you Lord.

"Take This Cup from Me"—letter dated November 1984

105

Fear of Not Meeting Deadlines – Letter-prayer dated November 1984

"Fear of Not Meeting Deadlines"—letter dated November 1984

December 1984

Dear Jesus:

I've been putting off approaching you in this manner as I find that I come to you mostly when I need something. This happens only because I'm weak, Lord.

Also I've become desperate as my funds are extremely low. I know that you have come to my assistance and aid so many, many times in the past Lord, for this I humbly tell you how thankful I am for your great mercy!

You once said, "Ask, and it shall be given you; seek and ye shall find, knock and it shall be opened unto you." Lord, I'm now knocking at your door, seeking your kind and merciful intervention in my life.

Also, Lord, I know that I should be patient and await your direction. I also know that you are looking after my welfare, but you know Lord that I'm weak, scared and worried. Most of all, Lord, you know that I am human and subject to human frailties.

Please Lord, give me the strength to be patient and calm, while I await your instructions and directions. Give me more faith, Lord, in this hour of need. Thank you, Lord, for everything.

"A Plea for Help and Strength"—letter dated December 1984

February 1985
Maryland, U.S.A.

Dear Lord:

The same way that I come to you for help, Sweet Jesus, I'm now coming to you in praise. You have been extremely kind and good to me in the past and even more recently. You continue to respond to my prayers, and to show me that you are really a Good Shepherd; a Good Samaritan; a tower of strength; a beacon in the dark; a caring Saviour; the outstretched hand in time of distress; a constant friend; companion and, indeed the Redeemer of mankind. Dear Lord, help me to seek you more often, and not only in times of distress and problems.

I thank you Lord for everything both great and small.

Amen + Amen.

"Thanksgiving Letter"—letter dated February 1985

Sources

Scriptural excerpts in this book are from -

The New Jerusalem Bible. Copyright ©1985 by Darton, Longman and Todd Ltd. and Doubleday, a division of Random House, Inc. Reprinted by Permission.

The Holy Bible, The New King James Version. Copyright ©1984 by Thomas Nelson Inc. Used by permission. All rights reserved.